Dear Dragon Developing Readers

Dear Dragon's Day at School!

by Marla Conn

Illustrated by Jack Pullan

NORWOOD HOUSE PRESS

NOTE TO CAREGIVERS: It is a pleasure to have the opportunity to adapt Margaret Hillert's **Dear Dragon** books for emergent readers! Children will grow and learn to read independently with the boy and his loveable pet dragon as they have done for over 30 years!

The new *Dear Dragon Developing Readers* series gives young children experiences with book concepts and print, and enables them to learn how language works; phonological awareness, letter formation, spaces, words, directionality and oral and written communication.

Emergent Readers are just beginning to control early reading behaviors and require books that have a high level of support including:

- Predictable & repeated language patterns
- Simple story lines
- Familiar topics & vocabulary

- Repetitive words and phrases
- Easy high frequency and decodable words
- Illustrations that support the text

We look forward to watching the lightbulb go on as emerging readers expand their literacy powers; building important strategies for maintaining fluency, correcting error, problem solving new words, and reading and writing for comprehension. The *Dear Dragon Developing Readers* will ultimately guide children through the more complex text in *Dear Dragon Beginning-to-Read Books* as they become curious, confident, independent learners.

Happy Reading!

Marla Con

Marla Conn, MS Ed.
Literacy Consultant/Author

Norwood House Press

For more information about Norwood House Press please visit our website at: www.norwoodhousepress.com or call 866-565-2900.

Copyright ©2022 by Norwood House Press. All rights reserved. Adapted from *Come to School, Dear Dragon* by Margaret Hillert. All rights reserved.

No part of this book may be reproduced or utilized in any form or by any means without written permission from the publisher.

Beginning-to-Read™ is a registered trademark of Norwood House Press.

LIBRARY OF CONGRESS CATALOGING–IN–PUBLICATION DATA

Names: Conn, Marla, author. | Pullan, Jack, illustrator. | Hillert, Margaret. Come to school, Dear Dragon.

Title: Dear Dragon's day at school! / by Marla Conn ; illustrated by Jack Pullan.

Description: Chicago : Norwood House Press, [2022] | Series: Dear Dragon developing readers | "Adapted from Come to school, Dear Dragon by Margaret Hillert." | Audience: Grades K-1. | Summary: "A boy's pet dragon visits him at school and joins the class in painting, reading, and playtime. An early emergent reader that includes a picture glossary, common sight words list, activities, and a note to caregivers"-- Provided by publisher.

Identifiers: LCCN 2021050232 (print) | LCCN 2021050233 (ebook) | ISBN 9781684508150 (hardcover) | ISBN 9781684046812 (paperback) | ISBN 9781684046959 (epub)

Subjects: LCSH: Readers (Primary) | Schools--Juvenile fiction. | Dragons--Juvenile fiction. | LCGFT: Readers (Publications)

Classification: LCC PE1119.2 .C66373 2022 (print) | LCC PE1119.2 (ebook) | DDC 428.6/2--dc23/eng/20211012

LC record available at https://lccn.loc.gov/2021050232

LC ebook record available at https://lccn.loc.gov/2021050233

Hardcover ISBN: 978-1-68450-815-0   Paperback ISBN: 978-1-68404-681-2

347N—012022

Manufactured in the United States of America in North Mankato, Minnesota.

WORDS IN THIS BOOK

PICTURE GLOSSARY:

 backpack

 book

 flag

 lunch box

 paintbrush

 playground

 school

 sign

 teacher

COMMON SIGHT WORDS:

- a
- I
- see

I see a backpack.

I see a lunch box.

I see a school.

I see a flag.

I see a teacher.

13

I see a paintbrush.

I see a book.

I see a playground.

19

I see a stop sign.

Word Work

Compound Words!

1. Discuss that compound words are two words put together to make a new word.

2. Go back to the story and find all the compound words.

   Back + pack =   Paint + brush =
   Lunch + box =   Play + ground =

3. Brainstorm compound words with the group. Create a compound word chart.

Activity

On a separate piece of paper, draw a picture to answer each question.

1. What does Dear Dragon take to school?

2. What does Dear Dragon see when he is in school?

3. Where does Dear Dragon go for recess?

4. Why does Dear Dragon see a stop sign?

About the Author

Marla Conn has been an educator and literacy specialist for over 30 years. Witnessing the amazing moment when the "lightbulb goes on" as young children process print and learn how to read independently inspired a passion for creating books that support aspiring readers. She has a strong belief that all children love stories and have a natural curiosity for books. Marla enjoys reading, writing, playing with her 2 golden doodles, and spending time with family and friends.

About the Illustrator

A talented and creative illustrator, Jack Pullan is a graduate of William Jewell College. He has also studied informally at Oxford University and the Kansas City Art Institute. He was mentored by the renowned watercolor artists, Jim Hamil and Bill Amend. Jack's work has graced the pages of many enjoyable children's books, various educational materials, cartoon strips, as well as many greeting cards. Jack currently resides in Kansas.